Messiah's Birth

Christy Warford
Illustrated by Karina Downer

Dedication

Grace Bible Church, thank you all for your encouragement when I decided to write this book, and for helping me to complete this project. May this book be an aid to all churches and their kiddos.

Karina, thank you for being willing to do these illustrations for me. Without you I would not have this complete project.

Note to parents

This book is intended as an aid to help tell the birth of Jesus. I have added definitions to help explain some of the more difficult terms.

There are questions at the end of every chapter. We should all be asking these sweet questions as we read God's Word. They are a tool to help train our children how to read God's Word and show what simple questions they can ask as they read. My children asked these questions, and I pray they will be a help to your children.

Table of Contents

Zechariah and Elizabeth

Luke 1:5-25

One day when Zechariah was doing his priestly duty, he was chosen to enter the temple to burn the incense offering. While he was performing his duties, an angel of the Lord came and stood before him. Fear took hold of Zechariah when he saw the angel. But the angel said to him, "'Do not be afraid, Zechariah, for your prayer has been heard, and your wife, Elizabeth, will bear you a son, and you will call his name John. And you will have joy and gladness, and many will rejoice at his birth.' He will be obedient to the Lord and will turn many of the sons of Israel back to the Lord their God. He will make the people ready for the Lord's coming."

Zechariah was unsure, "How will I know this for sure? I am way too old and so is my wife."

"'I am Gabriel, who stands before God, and I was sent to speak to you and to bring you this good news.' Because you did not believe these words, you shall not speak until your son is born," proclaimed Gabriel.

When Zechariah came out of the temple, he was unable to speak. Those who had been waiting for him to come out knew he had seen a vision in the temple because of how long he had been in the temple. He had been in there much longer than he should have been. Because Zechariah could not speak, he could not tell them what had happened.

Zechariah went home to Elizabeth once his time for his priestly duty was complete. Just as the angel had told Zechariah, his wife Elizabeth became pregnant in her old age. She stayed away from everyone for five months, rejoicing and thankful for the baby she was going to have.

Zechariah: A priest, chosen by God. His wife was named Elizabeth. They had no children and were too old to have children. They both loved God and obeyed God's commands. It had also been 400 years since God or His angels had spoken to anyone.

Priestly duty: The temple priests were divided into 24 groups who served in a rotation. Each group served twice a year in the temple doing the things God had told them to do in the book of Leviticus.

Incense offering: This was a special duty that not every priest would get to do. God would choose who would get to enter the temple each time to do this. The priest chosen would enter the temple to burn the incense offering to God, a pleasing aroma to Him. When a man was chosen, it was a very special and unique opportunity.

Questions

What did you learn about God in this story?

What did you learn about your heart?

Mary

Luke 1:26-38

In Elizabeth's sixth month of pregnancy, the angel, Gabriel was sent by God to a young girl named Mary. She was engaged to a godly man named Joseph. She was still a virgin and a descendant of King David. "Greetings, favored one! The Lord is with you."

Mary was shocked and puzzled. Gabriel quickly said, "'Do not be afraid, Mary, for you have found favor with God.' He has chosen you because of your faithfulness. You will become pregnant and have a baby boy. You will name Him Jesus. 'He will be great and will be called the Son of the Most High, and the Lord God will give Him the throne of His father David,' just as God has promised David. Jesus 'will reign over the house of Jacob forever,' and His kingdom will have no end."

"How can this be? I am not married and I am a virgin." Mary asked curious and confused.

"The Holy Spirit will come upon you, and the power of the Most High will overshadow you; and for that reason the holy Child shall be called the Son of God." Gabriel continued to tell Mary about her relative Elizabeth, Zechariah's wife, who was also going to have a baby boy in her old age.

Mary responded with joy. She was willing to obey God and do as He asked of her, "I am God's slave, may this happen just as you have said it would."

King David: Do you remember who he is? He is a very important part of God's plan. God made a promise to King David and it was about to be fulfilled. God called King David a man after God's own heart! King David also wrote a lot of the Psalms.

Descendant: Someone in the same family as someone else—a son, grandson, or great grandson and so on.

Questions

What did you learn about God in this story?

What did you learn about your heart?

Mary and Elizabeth

Luke 1:39-45

After Gabriel had come to Mary, she decided to go and visit her family, Zechariah and Elizabeth, and she was so excited for what God was doing, she wanted to see them. When Mary greeted Elizabeth, as soon as she arrived at Zechariah and Elizabeth's home, the baby inside of Elizabeth leaped at Mary's greeting!

Elizabeth, being filled with the Holy Spirit and joy, cried out in a loud voice and said to Mary, "You are blessed among women! The fruit of your womb is also blessed! 'And how has it happened to me, that the mother of my Lord would come to me? For behold, when the sound of your greeting reached my ears, the baby leaped in my womb for joy!' You are blessed because you believed what was spoken to you by the Lord."

Mary praised God for the many things He had done for His people, Israel. Mary, Elizabeth, and Zechariah were some of the few people in this time who truly loved the Lord and tried to bring Him glory in all that they did.

Mary stayed with Elizabeth and Zechariah for three months before returning home.

Questions

What did you learn about God in this story?

What did you learn about your heart?

John

Luke 1:57-80

When the time had come, Elizabeth gave birth to a son. Her neighbors and family rejoiced with her for the display of great mercy that God had given her.

"You should name him Zechariah, after his father," the family members and neighbors were telling Elizabeth after her son had been born.

Elizabeth replied, "No, he shall be called John."

Everyone, astonished and confused, said, "But there is no one in your family with that name." They turned to Zechariah and made signs to him about the name, for Zechariah still could not speak.

Zechariah made signs for them to get something for him to write on so that he could answer them. Quickly they got him something so he could write.

"His name shall be John," Zechariah wrote for everyone to read. At once Zechariah's mouth was opened and he could speak. The first thing that came out of his mouth was praise to God!

Everyone was amazed and astonished and fear came on them. "I wonder then, who will this child be?" they began asking one another.

Zechariah became filled with the Holy Spirit and began to prophesy. He prophesied about God and His goodness and for God's coming salvation for sinful men remembering the promise God gave to His people and Abraham.

He also prophesied that John would be called the prophet of the Most High and that he would go before the Lord to prepare the way. John would give people the knowledge of salvation by forgiveness of sins because of God's mercies.

Questions

What did you learn about God in this story?

What did you learn about your heart?

Joseph

Matt 1:18-25

When Joseph found out his soon-to-be wife was pregnant by the Holy Spirit, he planned to send Mary away secretly and not marry her. Joseph was a righteous man and did not want to bring shame on Mary.

While he was thinking about this, an angel of the Lord appeared to Joseph in a dream. "Joseph, do not be afraid to marry Mary. The child that she is pregnant with was conceived by the Holy Spirit, like she told you. Mary will have a Son and you will name Him Jesus. He is going to save His people from their sins."

Joseph awoke from his dream. He got up and did just as the angel had told him to do. He went and married Mary just as he had promised. Joseph kept Mary a virgin until after she gave birth to her Son.

Questions

What did you learn about God in this story?

What did you learn about your heart?

Jesus

Luke 2:1-7

A decree went out from Caesar Augustus, the ruler of the Roman Empire, to have a census taken of all the people in his land. Everyone had to travel to the original birthplace of their families to register for the census.

For Joseph and Mary, it meant they had to travel to Bethlehem as they were both descendants of King David who was from Bethlehem. At this time, they were living in the city of Nazareth. They had to travel about 70 miles to get to Bethlehem while Mary was at the end of her pregnancy.

It was a very hard journey through mountains with rocky and narrow roads. They had to go very slow because it was such a difficult road, especially for a pregnant woman.

Once they finally reached Bethlehem, the town was very crowded. Mary and Joseph began to go from one inn to the next trying to find a place to stay. They found all the rooms were already full.

One innkeeper decided to try to find a place for them. He took them to a stable where the animals were kept. With the inn being full, it was probably full also. But the innkeeper made room for Joseph and Mary at the stable. There Mary gave birth to a baby boy, just as God had promised. God had provided a place for them in a stable.

After giving birth, Mary took her baby, and wrapped him in cloths and laid him in a manger because there was nothing else to use as a bed for him. God's own son, the King born into humble means, was placed in the lowliest of places.

Census: Counting how many people live in a kingdom. Everyone needed to return to their ancestors' homeland.

Hospitals: There were no hospitals like we have today. Women delivered their babies at home.

Manger: Feeding trough for animals to eat their food. Usually about the size of a bassinet.

Questions

What did you learn about God in this story?

What did you learn about your heart?

The Shepherds

Luke 2:8-20

The same night, out in the fields, shepherds were watching over their sheep. Out of nowhere, an angel of the Lord stood before them. Then the glory of the Lord shone all around them. The shepherds were frightened.

"Do not be afraid! I bring you good news that will bring all people great joy. Today in the city of David, Bethlehem, 'there has been born for you a Savior, who is Christ the Lord. And this will be the sign for you: you will find a baby wrapped in cloths and lying in a manger.'"

Once the angel finished talking, suddenly there appeared a multitude of angels praising God and saying, "Glory to God in the highest, And on earth peace among men with whom He is pleased."

When the angels had left, the shepherds began talking to one another. "Let us go now to Bethlehem and see this thing 'which the Lord has made known to us.'" So they hurried to find Mary and Joseph.

When they arrived, they found everything to be just as the angels had said, a baby wrapped in cloths and laying in a manger.

The shepherds were amazed and told Mary and Joseph all about what the angel had said. Then the shepherds returned to their flocks praising God for all that He had allowed them to see and hear. All those who heard about these things from the shepherds were amazed.

Mary treasured all these things in her heart.

Questions

What did you learn about God in this story?

What did you learn about your heart?

Simeon
and Anna

Luke 2:21-38

Mary and Joseph named the baby boy Jesus, just as the angel had told them. When Jesus was eight days old, He was brought to the temple. Mary and Joseph brought Him to Jerusalem to present Him to the Lord, as God had commanded for all first-born boys.

Now there was a man in Jerusalem whose name was Simeon and he was a righteous man who loved God. The Holy Spirit was upon Simeon and had revealed to him that he would not see death before he had seen the Lord's Messiah. Joseph and Mary went into the temple to carry out the law with the baby boy, Jesus.

Simeon took Jesus in his arms and blessed God. "Now Master, You are releasing Your slave in peace, According to Your word. For my eyes have seen Your salvation, Which You prepared in the presence of all peoples, A LIGHT FOR REVELATION TO THE GENTILES, And for the glory of Your people Israel."

Joseph and Mary were amazed at the things that were being said about their little baby boy. Simeon blessed them and said to Mary, "Behold, this Child is appointed for the fall and rise of many in Israel, and for a sign to be opposed--and a sword will pierce through your own soul as well--that the thoughts from many hearts may be revealed."

Then a prophetess, Anna the daughter of Phanuel, of the tribe of Asher, who was rather old as well, came up to Jesus, after hearing Simeon's blessing on Him.

She gave thanks to the Lord, and spoke of Jesus to all those who looked for the redemption of Jerusalem. Anna was one of the few key witnesses blessed by God to understand the significance of Jesus' birth.

She too was very excited to see Jesus as she also, like Simeon, had hoped to see Him one day. She loved God and, being a widow, she had devoted her life to praying and fasting daily on the temple grounds where she chose to live not leaving the temple.

This was probably her only glimpse of Jesus, but it was enough for her to always be talking about Him to everyone she met.

Questions

What did you learn about God in this story?

What did you learn about your heart?

The Magi

Matt 2:1-23

When Jesus was born, God put a sign in the sky. Those men who had learned about the coming Son of God decided to go see Him for themselves. They were royal and traveled a great distance to see Jesus. It took them a few years to get to Jesus. There was a group of about 300 or so men. God had created a big, bright star that stood over where Jesus lived so they could find Him.

The magi went their way and found the Child. They followed the star that guided them to the place where the Child was. When they came to the house, they rejoiced with great joy. Going into the house, they saw the Child and Mary His mother and they fell to the ground and worshiped Jesus. They gave the boy gifts that were fit for a king. They gave Him gold, frankincense, and myrrh.

The magi were then warned by God in a dream not to return to King Herod. So the magi left and returned to their own country by another way.

After the magi had left, an angel of the Lord appeared to Joseph. The angel told him to get up and take the Child and His mother to Egypt and stay there until he was told to return because Herod was wanting to find the Child and kill Him.

Joseph obeyed and did what God told him to do. They made it safely to Egypt where they lived until it was safe to return to Israel.

King Herod became angry when he realized the magi had not returned to tell him where the Child was. He decided to have every male child two years and younger killed, according to the time that the magi had told him the star appeared.

Herod did not want anyone trying to take his place as king. He was afraid of the Child taking away his crown. This is why he had no intention to worship Jesus, but to kill Him instead. He was a very greedy man who hated God.

When Herod died, God sent an angel to Joseph in Egypt. The angel appeared to Joseph in a dream and said, "Get up. Take Mary and Jesus back to Israel, for those seeking Jesus' life are now dead."

Joseph obeyed and they returned to Israel. But when they returned, Joseph learned that Herod's son Archelaus was now ruling in his father's place.

Joseph became afraid to return to Bethlehem. God then warned Joseph in a dream not to return to the area of Bethlehem.

Joseph took his family back to Nazareth where Mary and Joseph had lived before the census. There Jesus grew up and became known as Jesus of Nazareth.

Magi: Jesus was born in the time when Herod the king ruled over Judea. The city of Bethlehem is in Judea. When Jesus was about two years old, He had some visitors come to see Him. Magi were men from the East. How did they know about Jesus? Well that is an easy answer. Back in the Old Testament, Israel disobeyed God. God had promised the Israelites if they would not obey, He would punish them. So He did. He sent them out of the Promised Land and into other lands far from their own country. Some of the Israelites still loved and obeyed God and they told the people of these new lands about the coming Messiah.

Questions

What did you learn about God in this story?

What did you learn about your heart?

◇

About the author

Christy Warford graduated from
The Master's College (now The Master's
University) in 2002 with a degree in History.

I have been married 20+ years and we have
three beautiful daughters that I homeschool.
Our family attends a new church plant from
Grace Bible Church in Tempe, AZ, Gilbert
Bible Church, in Gilbert, AZ.

I was born and raised in Arizona. When I
graduated from college, I said I wanted to be
a published author. God's plan was for me
to wait twenty plus years. Now I have this
book and one other, Eclipse's Decision. I
am continuing to write more stories and
hope to have them published.

About the Illustrator

Karina Downer graduated from The New York Academy of Art with a Masters in Fine Art.

As an Artist, I am enamored with light, but there is more to capture. While I enjoy painting landscapes, portraits, and everyday life, it is God's living word that truly enlightens.

My hope is to make art that reflects that love, art with beauty and purpose. I attend Grace Bible Church in Tempe, AZ with my husband, son, and daughter. You can find me at www.capturingdelight.com.

dc0df3bb-ab21-4209-b752-2aeb19f71ca7R01